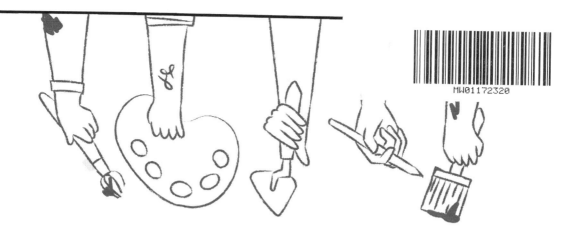

Hello Friend,

We are a group of passionate artists and designers
dedicated to providing practical and inspiring products to users.
With a focus on creating high-quality books for all ages,
we combine our love for drawing and design to produce exceptional creations.
Each member of us brings their unique talents and expertise,
resulting in a harmonious collaboration that results in beautifully intricate
illustrations and captivating designs.
With a deep commitment to our craft, Spark's Team aims to
ignite the creative spark within individuals and bring joy to your lives through
our thoughtfully crafted products.

Spark Team!

SCAN ME!
for more products

COLOR TEST PAGE

Thank you for your trust in us.

Our utmost desire is for you to experience immense joy
and satisfaction while using our one-of-a-kind designs.
If our book meets or exceeds your expectations, we
kindly ask you to take a moment and leave a review.
Your feedback serves as a constant source of
motivation for us to create even more remarkable books
in the future.
Thank you once again for your unwavering support.
We sincerely hope that our book will infuse your life
with a delightful blend of creativity and relaxation.

Made in the USA
Middletown, DE
13 October 2023

40765937R00060